CW01666854

LESSONS FROM AN UNEXPECTED JOURNEY

ESSENTIAL KEYS FOR OVERCOMING LIFE'S GREATEST CHALLENGES

BARRY AWOLUSI

AWOLUSI PUBLISHING

LESSONS FROM AN UNEXPECTED JOURNEY

Essential Keys For Overcoming Life's Greatest Challenges

A division of Awolusi Publishing

ISBN: 978-0-9935394-2-8

CONTENTS

ACKNOWLEDGMENTS

I would like to acknowledge the following important people in my life, those who supported me morally.

From my University Lectures: Deborah Caws, Dr. Tarisai Chilomba, Eddie Orija. ARU Wellbeing: Sarah Webber, Kelly Johnson, and my classmates Daniel Boateng, Christina Chidhakwa, and Rasia Malik. Grace Ndongwe, Christina Agbajobi, Oluwakemi Olorunfemi, and others whom I couldn't mention by name.

Special thanks to my nuclear family: my wife, Victoria; my children: Richard, Samuel, Comfort, Michael, Joy, my daughter in-law Molie and granddaughter Mila-Mary; my extended family and friends: Wale, Jo, and their children; Bose, Kisha, and her children; Uncle Bisi; Esther; Grace; Debbi; Daniel and his family; Bunmi Okeowo; my daughter, Tundun, and her husband, Mr. Ibrahim, and children; Enoch Abayomi; Yemi Gbadamosi; Gloria Bgadamosi; Ugozi Adda; Mimi Adda.

To my best friends: Austine Agwu, Dayo & Tina Gabrel and their children; Bishop Akinbiyi Akintola; Gbenga & Kemi Opatunde; Uncle Timothy Olla and their families; Mary Obikwu; Nora Igwu; Ugo; Remilekun Adenuga; Sister Bisi Bello and family; My publisher Joseph Ademosu and family; Dr. Ola; our special girl, Taiwo Siwoku, though she is not here with us (may her soul rest in peace); Granddad who has been praying for me.

I apologise if your name is not included; it was simply an oversight and I remain grateful to the part that you have played.

MY BEGINNING

Everyone has a beginning. Some emerge into this world amidst formidable setbacks, while others arrive with narratives that defy the ordinary, triumphing over supernatural forces and adversity. No matter how your journey began, it is and will always be a journey of significance because your life is a precious gift bestowed upon you by the Creator.

I come from a small town in Nigeria, Oke-Irunn in Ekiti, located in Ondo State, born on August 22nd, 1953. My late mother, Chief Mrs. Elizabeth Farounbe Sadat Awolusi, and father, Chief Samson Olode Awolusi, have both passed away. I am the youngest among eight siblings, consisting of five boys and three girls, with only my sister and I remaining. My mother lived to the remarkable age of 120 years and 9 months, while my father passed away at 58. Despite the adversities, my mother led a fulfilling life, leaving behind a legacy of wisdom and compassion, having witnessed four generations of her descendants.

Growing up was tough as my mother had to single-handedly care for eight children, resorting to various means of survival such as selling food and handmade clothes. I vividly remember my childhood days selling food after school in our close-knit community where everyone knew each other. Unfortunately, I faced bullying at school for helping my mother and struggled academically due to undiagnosed dyslexia. Unable to afford shoes, I would make slippers from car tires both to wear and sell to my peers. Even with the financial hardships, I displayed a knack for craftsmanship, quickly mastering the art of basket making. However, the bullying persisted, leading to frequent altercations both at school and home and I became increasingly aggressive. Each day seemed to bring a new fight, often, to my mother's dismay, resulting in me returning home with a bloodstained school uniform. My anger stemmed from frustration, as I struggled to concentrate in class and found the schoolwork challenging. At the time, I was unaware that dyslexia and (ADHD) was the underlying cause of my difficulties. At the age of eight, I was taken in by my sister and her husband Mr and Mrs Olaleye.

My brother-in-law was a kind-hearted man, he was a blessing, very nice, honest, and loved by everyone. My sister, on the other hand, was strict and we didn't get along very well. During the four to five years I spent with them, my sister made me do everything—from washing clothes and fetching fresh water from the river to collecting firewood and cooking. When I'd refuse to do housework, it would mean no food for me that day, so when I went to the farm to collect firewood to sell, I'd also hunt for bush meat to eat.

In spite of the support of my brother-in-law, life remained arduous, marked by laborious chores and constant hunger. Yet, amidst the struggles, there were moments of relief, such as the incident involving a snake and a water-fetching mishap. I often found solace in playing with snakes. Sometimes, I would bring them home as pets or use them to scare my classmates who mistreated me. It didn't entirely stop the bullying, but it lessened it somewhat.

One day, my niece demanded I fetch water about two miles away from home, alone. I was angry with her, but I knew refusing would result in a beating and no food. Along the way, I encountered a big snake, which I killed and put inside the bucket with the water I had collected.

Upon returning home, I found my niece waiting for the water. Delighted to see her, I asked for her help with the bucket. As she tried to assist me, I deliberately tilted the bucket, causing the water and snake to spill onto her. I quickly picked the dead snake up chasing her with it as she ran screaming. Even with the initial shock, we turned the incident into a joke within the household. From that day forward, nobody ever sent me alone to fetch water!

When I was 12 years old, my brother, Brother Ade, extended an invitation for me to come to Lagos, but I couldn't read a single word of his letter. I sought the help of my friend, Francis Oke, who read it aloud to me. However, when one of my schoolmates snatched and tore the letter in disbelief, assuming I wouldn't actually go, I reacted impulsively, biting and injuring him. Consequently, he missed school for a few days, and his parents confronted mine.

I received a scolding at home, but it didn't bother me much as I had my eyes set on Lagos Nigeria. Unable to face my sister, I turned to my brother-in-law who believed my every word. He generously provided the money for my journey to Lagos, advising me to behave and not inform my sister about my permanent stay there.

In those days, I was forbidden from entering my father's house due to my volatile behaviour, so once I arrived in Lagos, I stayed with my brother, Folu, who was initially kind and caring. At the time I was with him, I called him Dad. There was a part of me that had begun to genuinely see my brother as my father. I believe this stemmed from a subconscious longing and necessity for a paternal presence in my life as a child. He fulfilled all the roles and responsibilities I associated with a father figure, and I cherished him as such. However, everything changed when his wife revealed to me that I wasn't his biological child, this led to a strained relationship with my brother's wife until I left Nigeria.

Around the age of 12 or 13, my brother Folu enrolled me in a local school where my sister-in-law, Mrs. Adedapo, served as the head teacher. Unbeknownst to my brother, I struggled with reading and writing. During a placement test at the school, I confessed my difficulties to Mrs. Adedapo, filled with dread. She reassured me and promised to speak with my brother Folu about it. The day passed in anxious anticipation, and eventually, Mrs. Adedapo invited my brother over, sensing my distress. After a lengthy discussion between them, my brother informed me of my new path: learning motorcycle mechanics as an apprentice. I was initially reluctant but began my apprenticeship immediately, spending over a year honing my skills. Whilst I didn't see it at the time, looking back I can see how pivotal this opportunity was. My intelligence wasn't lacking; rather, my method of learning differed. Back in those days, they did not have the knowledge or resources that are now made available to those with dyslexia, ADHD and other learning difficulties. The apprenticeship offered me the chance to showcase my abilities in a way that suited my learning style.

One afternoon, as usual at the mechanic shop, my boss gave me money to purchase lunch for everyone. As I made my way back, I unexpectedly bumped into a slightly older female schoolmate who greeted me enthusiastically. Overwhelmed with shyness, I struggled to respond when she inquired about my choice of profession, in that moment I felt the same way I usually felt when in the classroom. Even though it could not be further from the truth I felt small, inadequate and foolish. Frustrated with my inability to articulate my feelings, I threw away the lunch and returned home rather than going back to work. Meanwhile, my boss, unable to locate me, visited my brother's office to lodge a complaint.

When I arrived home, my brother noticed my demeanour and demanded an explanation. Reluctantly, I recounted the events, resulting in his disappointment and a stern scolding. Regardless of my actions, he later approached me with an offer to work in his photography studio, which I gladly accepted. Over the following months, I honed my skills, attracting more clients and even accompanying my brother on various assignments. We covered weddings and sporting events, capturing memorable moments and earning a substantial income.

. . .

THE STRUGGLES OF MY YOUTH

I never really knew my father and the uncertainty surrounding my lack of relationship with him weighed heavily on me and greatly impacted what I believed about my identity and capabilities. I would visit my mother when possible, during a visit she confided in me, expressing remorse for directing her frustrations towards me and revealing details about our father's character. Touched by her words, I apologised for my actions and sought to begin mending our relationship, yearning to understand my past and my absent father.

Shame is a heavy weight that will prevent you from moving forward. It always hinders progress. Whenever we carry shame, everything is harder, more complex and the triumphs and wins of life are difficult to fully embrace. The feeling of inadequacy weighed heavily on me for the first twenty-two years of my life, ensnaring me in its grip. Reflecting on my past, I realise that shame had always been a constant companion that haunted me even from my earliest memories.

I felt its sting with every rejection, each instance reinforcing feelings of worthlessness and insignificance. It whispered in my ear when I endured abuse in silence, convincing me it was my own fault. Shame lurked in the shadows as I tried to conceal my true self, constantly apologising, downplaying my abilities, or striving to overcompensate for a self-perceived sense of inferiority.

Have you experienced it too? If you're human, undoubtedly you have, and the outcome is always the same – shame diminishes us, brands us as flawed and unworthy under its influence. Shame breeds a fear of unworthiness, poisoning our relationships with God, ourselves, and others, hindering our ability to embrace and extend God's boundless love.

Yet, it was through God's immense love, that I began to grasp the power of His Word to dismantle the lies I once believed and uncover the truth of my identity and purpose. But, let it be known, this journey remains ongoing—it's not a swift fix or an instant remedy. Instead, it's a profound, continuous exploration of God's love and his transformative power. Even now, after all this time, I continue to unearth deeper revelations, knowing the process won't conclude until I stand before Him. And I wouldn't want it any other way.

In my life, God has been weaving a remarkable narrative, demonstrating His ability to liberate and uplift a once-shamed man into a cherished son, a vessel of His Spirit, and an integral part of His redemptive work in our broken world. He desires the same for you. God crafted you with a unique purpose, a specific plan, and a mighty destiny waiting to be fulfilled, but here's the good news — shame holds no sway over that purpose, plan, or destiny because Jesus came to set you free from its chains.

The sole pathway to obtaining, inheriting, and realising the promises of God, whether they be words, goals, plans, dreams, or visions nestled within our hearts, is through the twin virtues of faith and patience, as conveyed in Hebrews: We do not want you to become lazy, but to imitate those who through faith and patience inherit what has been promised.

(Hebrews 6:12).

Perhaps you have a dream, a goal, or a plan that you've diligently pursued for years, yet it feels as though God has forsaken you. Rest assured; God has not forgotten you. The dreams, visions, and plans instilled by God in our hearts demand time – ample time. Throughout this journey called life, if we surrender, God will actively begin shaping us inwardly, preparing us for His divine purposes. Our task is to exercise unwavering faith and enduring patience.

Faith involves believing in God's character and His fidelity to His promises, trusting that He is true to His word. Patience, on the other hand, involves enduring delays and waiting expectantly, confident in God's goodness, wisdom, and sovereignty, regardless of the duration or the purpose of the waiting. Faith is the boat that takes us to our destination and patience resembles the waves we ride on until we get there. We stand on patience until we tangibly receive the promise.

We are all summoned to embrace the unexpected, and it invariably demands faith to navigate through it. Yet, as we advance in faith, God unfailingly contends for us and orchestrates the miraculous. Let us acknowledge His interventions, the doors He opens, and the path He lays before us, recognising His supernatural intervention in our lives. Though His methods may not align with our expectations, He unfailingly honours our obedience. In my own journey, every miraculous occurrence unfolded after stepping out in faith and obedience, I positioned myself to be willing, entrusting myself wholly to Him.

Though I may not know your specific calling or destiny, I am confident that you possess greatness within you because our Creator has a good plan for your future. At every crossroad in your journey, you will encounter daunting challenges, with a choice to either recoil in fear or advance in faith. One option will confine you to your present circumstances, while the other will propel you toward your destined future. You can delve deeper into your destiny and have a clearer understanding of your purpose from a place of peace and unwavering trust in God, even amidst life's unforeseen twists and turns, by simply seeking Him.

There were times in my life when I felt utterly hopeless, and it was as if everything and everyone were conspiring against me. I was convinced that without education, reaching the pinnacle of success was impossible. However, I've come to realise that this notion couldn't be further from the truth. Success knows no boundaries, and it hinges on several factors:

1. Your location: Where you are is important, your success will be linked to a specific place and a specific people.

2. The company you keep: Those that are closest to you provide a snapshot of who you are and who you will be.

3. Vision: To realise anything in life you need to see it with your heart first – vision is seeing with the heart, having foresight and insight of a future that goes beyond the limits of your present reality.

4. Determination: You must have a strong purpose and firm resolve to achieve success and overcome obstacles when they arise. Successful people make quality decisions.

5. Passion: Passion is the attitude that will propel you into a world of success, it is a posture that positions you on a trajectory of onwards and upwards.

6. Self-belief: If you fail to believe in what you are doing then it is unlikely others will. One of the most important relationships in your life is the one you have with yourself – invest in you and others will too.

There are countless uneducated individuals who have amassed great wealth and success worldwide. If you're reading this and have been influenced by the negativity propagated by teachers, family, or friends, let this book serve as a beacon of encouragement. You are not a failure. Do you know that remaining in poverty is a choice? I can say that with confidence because I've witnessed individuals born in the depths of poverty rise to prominence through sheer hard work. Your beginning does not have to be your end, you can write a different story and change your ending irrespective of how things may have started. Nothing can permanently hinder you except your own limitations.

I recall one of my nephews sharing a story about a man who embarked on a business venture at the age of 67 and became a multimillionaire. This anecdote inspired me as I contemplated my retirement and sought part-time employment. While God would often bless me with business ideas, I would always await the opportune moment to execute them. Soon enough, inspiration struck, leading me to embark on the journey of publishing my first book titled "Anybody Can Be A Father But It Takes A Special Person To Be A Dad.

It was a challenging endeavour, fraught with moments of discouragement. However, with the divine intervention of God and the unwavering support of significant individuals in my life, including my mentor, a sister in the Lord, Lizzy Amosan, my daughter in Christ, Sandra Mighty, Bishop Akinbiyi Akintola, my brother Timothy Olla, and most notably, my dear wife, I persevered. My wife, in particular, went above and beyond, utilising her savings to assist in funding the publication of the book. I know only too well that behind every successful man stands a kind-hearted, blessed woman.

The journey of self-publishing was far from easy, it was a ten-year process as there were times of self-doubt and numerous setbacks. Whilst losing my notes multiple times and facing pressures about the release of a second book, I remained steadfast in my vision to complete my first book by 2017 by God's grace. A trip I took to Nigeria was instrumental in providing the conducive environment to continue writing. Amidst the hectic pace of life at home, balancing family responsibilities, ministry commitments, and writing proved to be a challenge. This was all exacerbated by my wife's health struggles, which eventually resulted in the relinquishment of my business in 2007.

At times, I found myself questioning God and the fairness of our circumstances, but His response reminded me of the promise that He works all things together for good, for those who love Him and are called according to His purpose (Romans 8:28). I contemplated cancelling my trip to Nigeria, but soon found solace in knowing that I could draw strength from God's grace. I write this filled with gratitude for the journey thus far and for God's continued grace and strength. Irrespective of any obstacles, I press on, trusting that God will always see me through. Even with the periods of questioning and doubt, I've found solace in God's love and because of that, in my darkest moments, I've persevered, confidently knowing God has a plan for me.

A TURNING POINT

The turning point in my life came unexpectedly when one day a friend of mine, Tunde Soyemi, asked me if I wanted to go to Technical College?

Without fully understanding the significance of my response, I hastily agreed. The college was in Abeokuta, Ogun State, Nigeria. In the following days, as the reality sank in, I found myself questioning my decision. I was faced with inner turmoil, unable to confide in anyone, not even my girlfriend at the time, Sade Abebi, whom I had met a few months prior.

As the day approached and it was time to travel to the college, Tunde proved to be a true blessing. He is a reserved yet remarkably intelligent individual, who became a pivotal figure in my life. Though we have not crossed paths in over 25 years, I still hold him in high regard, viewing him as an angel sent to guide me.

Upon arriving at the college, I was granted admission after a brief interview. Despite my joy, anxiety gnawed at me as

I worried about how to cope with the challenges ahead, including financing my education. My relationship with my brother Folu was strained, adding to my worries.

Upon returning to Lagos, I shared the good news with Sade but kept my struggles and worries hidden. The years at the college, from 1974 to 1979, were marked by hardship. However, with divine intervention and the support of individuals like Ayo Adetutu, a classmate whose exceptional intelligence inspired me, I began to overcome every obstacle. Within a year, I gained the ability to read and write proficiently, and a miraculous restoration of my memory of things I had learned previously.

My family, initially sceptic of my college enrolment, eventually celebrated my achievements. I did not succeed alone. My girlfriend contributed to my tuition and ensured I had necessities, while my brother stepped in to cover the final year's expenses. Their support, coupled with my determination to succeed and provide for my mother, which was a promise I had made to her, propelled me forward.

In retrospect, I consider myself immensely blessed and fortunate to have embarked on this journey of self-discovery and growth. Determination proved to be the key to my breakthrough, enabling me to overcome setbacks and fulfil my responsibilities with gratitude to God.

JOURNEY THROUGH EDUCATION

After completing my college education, I secured a job at UTC Motors as an Assistant Technical Officer, earning a substantial salary of 250 Naira per month - an amount that held significant value for me and anyone with similar qualifications at the time. After nine months, I transitioned to a job at the University of Lagos as a Technical Officer, moving closer to home.

In January 1974, while at the bank to collect my salary, I encountered my uncle, Professor Adeyemo. After exchanging greetings, we engaged in a lengthy conversation during which he inquired about my pursuits. Upon learning about my aspirations, he proposed the idea of furthering my education abroad. Given the opportunity through his wife's role as Commissioner for Education Scholarship Board, he provided me with a note to present to her. The following day, accompanied by my friend Gbenga Opatunde, we visited her office. Each of us was given a form to fill out, which we promptly completed and returned. Two weeks later, we were summoned for an interview, both of us emerging successful. In May, Gbenga departed for Nigeria to pursue studies in Electronic Engineering, while I embarked on a journey to Romania to pursue studies in Automobile Engineering.

In October 1979, I left Nigeria for Romania to pursue a degree in Automobile Engineering. Reflecting on my experiences during my college years and at the university in Romania, I recall facing difficulties and enduring bullying from peers. However, I emerged stronger, driven by the belief that the trials I faced were a small price to pay for the eventual rewards. Transitioning from a background devoid of secondary school education to becoming a successful businessman, pilot, engineer, author, and, above all, a devoted family man was not attributable to luck but to the goodness of God and my unwavering dedication.

Even though my time in Romania was filled with challenges of racism and prejudice, I discovered that adversity did not necessarily mean the end. I had learned to stay hopeful and received invaluable assistance that helped me through. Subsequently, I journeyed to England in the early 1980s with a friend I met in France, where I then met Leslie, who informed us of his plans to study in London. Together, we embarked on this new chapter. Often, the people you come across in life can be used as agents of change to assist in taking you to the next level. Throughout my college and post-college years, I consistently encountered individuals divinely appointed to assist me, ensuring that favour was never far from reach. Each time I faced adversity, a breakthrough followed, underscoring the enduring presence of divine intervention. Even amidst my struggles with communication during my college years, I received support from friends, such as Gbenga Opatunde, who secured a summer job for me at Texaco Oil Company. In spite of the language barriers, I persevered, fulfilling simple tasks like bookkeeping.

There was a lot of support that I did not receive as a child, this motivated me to ensure things would be different for my own family when the time came. My vision has always been to achieve success in life and to demonstrate to my children that obstacles such as disability or lack of education need not impede one's path to success or prevent the provision of perennial care.

I share these stories with the belief that within them, you will discover echoes of your own experiences. I hope these anecdotes, drawn from my everyday life, reveal the hidden sparks of hope and redemption that permeate ordinary existence, resonating with everyone who reads about them.

Even though I have experienced numerous trials, I remain steadfast in the knowledge that my journey is far from over until God decrees otherwise. Each challenge I encountered served as a steppingstone, equipping me with the resilience needed to navigate life's complexities. Even though I had experienced a lack of parental guidance, I learned to cherish my wife and children, drawing upon my own experiences of poverty to empathies with others facing similar struggles.

My journey has been filled with unexpected twists and turns, but no matter how rough the road, perseverance always pays off. The key to success lies in staying committed and persistent. Arriving in the UK with only five pounds in my pocket, I didn't know a soul. When I arrived, I took shelter at a church in Elephant and Castle, where I stayed for a few days. Fortunately, a fellow travellers met a friend at Victoria station, a kind soul named Kunle Dagbo. He graciously offered us accommodation for a month and even took us to the job centre to seek employment. The rest, as they say, is history.

LOVES TRIUMPH

My plans to find a job in Nigeria were met with obstacles, leading me to return to London. During my absence, I discovered that Sade, my former girlfriend in Nigeria, had gotten into another relationship and was pregnant causing me great disappointment. My family initially believed that the baby was mine and had tried to support and look after her whilst I was away. It soon came to light what had actually happened but I could no longer continue the relationship. Although we had been together for over 12 years, she had betrayed me in a way that meant things could never be the same again.

I met my wife, Victoria, at her friend's house in Southwest London in 1984 during a summer party. It was a vibrant Saturday night, and amidst the festivities, I spotted a beautiful young woman. After sharing a dance, we stepped out onto the balcony to catch some fresh air and began talking. I was instantly captivated by her and told her that I loved her and wanted to marry her! Regardless of her initial shock, it was a moment of the beginnings of love at first sight for both of us.

However, shortly after, a friend warned me that she was still in school, which discouraged me. In response to this news, I distanced myself from Victoria for a few months. Eventually, my cousin encouraged us to reconcile, and we began spending time together again. Our bond grew stronger with each passing day, and we soon became inseparable.

At the time, I was a student at Redhill College of Aeronautic Engineering, while Victoria worked and attended Waltham Forest College in East London. Though we had different paths, we made time to see each other every weekend, forging a deep connection. Over time, even my friends who initially discouraged me from pursuing her grew fond of her. Months later, Victoria introduced me to her older sister, and our relationship continued to blossom.

I've been vocal about the goodness of God, which is evident in every facet of my life. However, I can't overlook the problems that arose from the difficulties I faced. When you lack understanding of your true identity and purpose, you inevitably adopt a false persona that does not reflect the wonderful individual God created you to be. My struggles led me into a downward spiral of depression and attempts to self-medicate with alcohol. Unfortunately, alcohol made a bad situation and exacerbated my depression instead of alleviating it.

During my time in Nigeria, I found myself sinking into depression and heavily relying on alcohol. My life felt chaotic, and upon returning to London, I struggled to find direction. Thankfully, with the support of friends like Kay Oluyemi, Samuel Ojo, Duro Lawal, and many others, I began to pick myself up and search for employment. Victoria stood by me, she supported me through my struggles with depression and drinking - providing unwavering encouragement, for which I am immensely grateful.

Soon after, Victoria discovered she was pregnant and I was overjoyed. I vividly remember celebrating in the hospital, though her initial visit was not for a pregnancy test. I was elated, jumping up and down in the hospital. Victoria had a more sober response. As we were not yet married, she feared her parents' reaction, particularly her father's, but I resolved to speak to him myself. From the moment I was introduced to Victoria's father, he took a liking to me, embracing me as part of the family. In spite of his no-nonsense demeanour and protective nature, he showed genuine warmth and acceptance which brought great comfort to me.

Victoria confided in her sister and mother, sharing her fear of facing her father. Determined to address the situation head-on, I soon approached her father and shared the news. To my relief, he welcomed the prospect of a second grandchild with open arms, surprising everyone in the family. We went on to share the good news with other family and friends, who celebrated the joyous occasion with us.

I later spoke to my father-in-law about the possibility of Victoria moving in with me in Hackney. However, he firmly stated that his daughter wouldn't live with any man without the commitment of marriage. Acknowledging his stance, I discussed the matter further with Victoria, contemplating our options. We wanted to marry and knew that we would eventually, but money was an issue. With neither of us financially stable at the time, I took it upon myself to seek employment. Registering at a mini-cab office in Brixton, I purchased a car and worked tirelessly, often sacrificing sleep and personal comfort to make ends meet and save for our wedding and future.

Reflecting on my wedding day in February 1986, I've learned that success isn't solely determined by background or circumstance but by trusting in God's plan. With wedding plans in motion, even with financial difficulties, we worked tirelessly to prepare for our wedding day. With the help of loyal friends, like my best man, Niyi Ogun, we managed to arrange a beautiful ceremony. Even though we lacked resources for a honeymoon, throughout it all, we leaned on our faith and each other, knowing that together, we could overcome any obstacle.

At the time of our wedding, I could only afford a ring for my soon-to-be-wife. I am reminded of the enduring love and resilience that has sustained our marriage for over thirty years. We have weathered many storms, yet our bond remains unshakable—a testament to the enduring power of love amidst adversity. In contrast, I have witnessed some of the most extravagant weddings result in marriages that falter within a matter of weeks because material wealth does not maintain or sustain a lasting relationship.

What unfolded in the years following our marriage was unforeseen—the good, the bad, and the ugly. Just six months after our wedding, we welcomed our first child, Richard, into the world. His arrival brought immense joy to our lives. However, on New Year's Eve 1986, while returning from church with my mother-in-law, Richard experienced a sudden seizure. As young parents, we were perplexed and initially attributed it to the warmth inside the car amidst the cold and snowy weather. Several days later, doctors diagnosed him with epilepsy, and for years, he endured frequent seizures, causing damage to his brain.

Richard attended nursery school but was later transferred to Whitefield School in Walthamstow, a special education school, due to his violent episodes. Dissatisfied with his progress there, we moved him to St. John's Primary School in Chigwell, Essex. However, one day, when returning home from school, Richard experienced a severe outburst, prompting us to seek urgent medical attention. This incident led to a prolonged hospital stay, during which we witnessed inadequate care and decided to advocate for his release.

Irrespective of our efforts, Richard's condition worsened, and he eventually lost his ability to speak. Social services advised us to place him in a residential care facility, where he remained for eight months, exhibiting violent behaviour. Reluctantly, we agreed, as we realised the toll it was taking on our family.

The situation took a similar turn five years later when our daughter, Comfort, began exhibiting similar symptoms. Like Richard, she spent eight months in the hospital, facing an unknown illness that baffled medical professionals. Born prematurely, Comfort initially showed no signs of illness but later developed concerning behaviours in school. Even with numerous medical interventions, her condition remained unexplained.

The burden placed on our family has been overwhelming, and we have sought solace in prayer and support from our community. It pains me to recount these experiences, but I feel compelled to share our journey, hoping to shed light on the challenges families like ours face. Though the road ahead may seem daunting, we remain steadfast in our faith and determination to overcome whatever obstacles come our way. Through it all, we have remained resilient. Through the setbacks and disappointments, we have persevered, guided by our unwavering trust in God. And though our path may not have been easy, we are grateful for the love and support that has sustained us along the way.

In May 2000, Victoria was involved in an accident in Epping Forest, Essex and five years later, she began experiencing difficulty walking. Doctors advised us to consider a back operation as her condition worsened. Following the first operation, while Victoria was recovering, she developed deep vein thrombosis (DVT), a condition that posed a severe risk to her life. This complication affected her heart, leading to a year-long stay at a special heart hospital. Even after being discharged and returning to work, Victoria's pain persisted, prompting further medical evaluations.

Life took a drastic turn, leaving me at a crossroads. I faced a pivotal choice: allow my circumstances to dictate my future happiness, or intentionally cultivate positivity and refuse to succumb to negativity. It was a decision of paramount importance.

Between 2000 and 2007, Victoria endured multiple issues, including another failed operation and subsequent complications. In 2007, during a nine-week hospitalisation, I made the difficult decision to close our business due to the strain it placed on our family and finances. Although it was painful to witness over twenty-six years of hard work go down the drain, prioritising my family's well-being was paramount. During this period, I experienced profound isolation as I navigated the complexities of caring for Victoria and our children while managing the closure of our business.

Following twenty-six years of business endeavour, the closure brought overwhelming heartache and devastation. In the aftermath, tears and negative thoughts inundated my days. The vision I held for the future vanished instantly, replaced by mounting losses and uncertainties. Fears about the unknown future compounded, especially concerning my children and the impact of their parents' separation on their well-being.

Day by day, negativity, hopelessness, and fear permeated deeper into my being, like a relentless whirlpool dragging me down. At times, the weight of my thoughts bordered on depression. Yet, amid this turmoil, a realisation dawned upon me.

Several months later, amidst emotional and mental exhaustion, I grew weary of despair. I refused to resign myself to sadness and hopelessness, recognising the need to model resilience for my children. I understood that my attitude would shape theirs, for better or worse. Trusting in God became my anchor, a source of peace and joy amid adversity.

I resolved not to dwell in bitterness or negativity, determined to embrace optimism and positive thinking despite the challenges. Surrendering negativity lightened my heart, and I discovered the power within me, through Christ, to choose positivity no matter the circumstances. With intentional effort, my perspective transformed, although my circumstances remained unchanged.

Reflecting on the past, I embraced the reality that yesterday is gone, and today is all I have. Thoughts of the future, especially concerning my children, occupied my mind. Amidst this, my wife's depression and violent outbursts as a result of her chronic back pain and her strained relationships with family members compounded her struggles.

With every hurdle I held onto hope, knowing that breakthroughs are always possible with God. Writing, especially during moments of sadness, brings relief and a semblance of joy. Though the journey ahead remains uncertain, I find solace in faith and the catharsis of expressing my thoughts on paper.

BACK HOME IN LONDON

Life is akin to a roller coaster, with its highs and lows. But what do you do when you find yourself in the valley of life, feeling lost and hopeless? When even your closest friends and family seem to turn their backs on you, and the prospects of employment and financial stability dwindle?

I've been there, witnessing the stark reality of life without financial security - times of unemployment, my wife's serious illness, and the necessity of relying on government benefits to make ends meet. I detested the idea of depending on benefits to provide for my family. Yet, when faced with the harsh truth of survival, I had no choice but to swallow my pride and accept assistance.

Now, in my retirement, I reflect on a career marked by brief job stints and recurring periods of financial instability. Although I was earning a meagre monthly income from pension benefits, it wasn't merely the financial strain that weighed heavily on me; it was the frustration and depression that accompanied it. My unhappiness permeated through my family, and witnessing their distress only added to my own.

But amidst the turmoil, I refused to succumb to despair. Giving up was not an option. However, thoughts of my age often plagued my mind, especially when job applications went unanswered, leaving me to question how much time was left before complete retirement.

My faith continues to sustain me through each trial. Daily prayers and meditation provide solace, reassuring me that everything will eventually fall into place. Recently, I attempted to become a driving instructor, only to fail the exam - a setback that left me feeling disheartened. Yet, after seeking solace in prayer and reflection, I found renewed hope.

Another challenge I faced was the absence of intimacy in my marriage due to my wife's illness. Our sex life dwindled, with intimacy becoming a rare occurrence. Even though she received medical assistance, I struggled with guilt and empathy, unable to fulfil all her needs while witnessing her suffering.

With hopes of things improving, upon my return from a trip, I found my wife's condition to be even worse than when I had left London. Just two days after my arrival, I promptly contacted our family doctor to schedule an appointment. At the clinic, she was examined and diagnosed with an infection from the injection she had received during a minor operation. She was prescribed antibiotics for a few days and referred back to the hospital.

A week later, we visited Queen's Hospital, where the orthopaedist informed us that the initial diagnosis was incorrect. It was her spine that required attention. After undergoing an X-ray, we were advised to book an MRI screening. Upon my return from Africa, I hardly had a good night's sleep, but I managed to work a few days.

To add to our family's difficulties, the lady who had been assisting my wife, and occasionally staying at our house, was also diagnosed with cancer on December 13th, 2016. This news was a tremendous shock to both our families. I accompanied her to the hospital for various tests and examinations. She has already undergone five rounds of chemotherapy and is progressing well, all thanks to God.

One key takeaway from this journey is the importance of finding joy in both good and bad times. It's crucial to maintain integrity and believe in oneself, regardless of the circumstances. Instead of dwelling on past failures, focus on positive change and trust in God's plan. Failure should never be viewed as final; rather, it's an opportunity for growth and resilience.

As King David wisely said, "I will wait till my change comes." It's essential not to lose hope and bury oneself in despair prematurely. Believe in yourself, for if you don't, no one else will. Sometimes, trials test our patience, but it's important to persevere and remain positive. Life is a journey with its ups and downs; therefore, it's vital to cherish every moment and celebrate both the highs and lows along the way.

Despite attempts to remain composed, the weight of our circumstances often felt overwhelming. However, through faith and perseverance, I found solace in knowing that our struggles were temporary and that brighter days lay ahead.

In writing this book, I aim to shed light on some of the challenges faced by families dealing with unexpected health crises and financial setbacks. I hope to offer encouragement to those grappling with similar trials, reminding them that they are not alone, and that resilience can emerge even in the darkest of times. Ultimately, no matter the hardships endured, I remain grateful for the opportunity to priorities my family's well-being and to face life's issues with unwavering determination.

A SEASON OF HOPELESSNESS

We all go through moments where we feel hopeless but there are, unfortunately for some, periods where it seems as though things will never change, and hopelessness becomes the norm. There came a time in my life when despair seemed to engulf me. Each day {I} felt like an uphill battle as I grappled with the weight of my responsibilities. With my wife hospitalised for nine weeks and our business in decline, I found myself overwhelmed by the trials that surrounded me. I have a typically outgoing nature, but often sat alone in the evenings, pondering when relief would arrive.

Deep down I held onto the belief that things would improve eventually, but at the time it was difficult to see a way out of the darkness. It felt like there was no light because I had become fixated on the darkness. People offered words of encouragement, assuring me that this difficult season would pass, but their reassurances provided little comfort in the depths of my despair.

It was only by the grace of God I was able to emerge from that bleak period. Whenever I witness others facing their own struggles with hopelessness, whether it's a husband losing his wife to cancer, a single mother unable to afford food, or a young person battling anxiety, I see the pain and uncertainty that many endure – because I was once there. I encourage others to cling to the hope that can only be found in God's Word, even in the darkest of times, knowing that His grace is sufficient for every trial and through every season.

In reflecting on my own journey, I've learned valuable lessons where perseverance and dedication often lead to success. Similarly, in both business and family life, it's important not to abandon ship when faced with temporary storms. Problems come but they also go, and with determination and resilience, we can weather any challenge. It was with the intention of offering hope to those who read it that I penned this book. If you find yourself in a place of hopelessness, overwhelmed by the challenges you face, I encourage you to seek solace in the promises of God. Remember, you are not a failure until you give up.

My family is a source of immense joy and fulfilment in my life, and I cherish them above all else. Although I grew up without the support of my parents, I've chosen to love and care for my children, recognising that they are not to blame for the circumstances they were born into. It saddens me to see that many in subsequent generations place less emphasis on family, prioritising quick wealth and material possessions over lasting relationships. However, I remain hopeful that by sharing my experiences, I can inspire others to value the importance of family and the responsibilities that come with it.

Everyone faces their own trials and tribulations, whether in family life, work, or health. I've made many mistakes in my life, but I have no regrets. I can say that with confidence because I've used past failures as steppingstones to growth, doing my best to provide for my children and impart wisdom to them. We are not all called to be millionaires and while not everyone will achieve huge financial wealth, it's important to find contentment with what we have.

FEELINGS OF INADEQUACY

When grappling with feelings of hopelessness and worthlessness, it's crucial to recall these essential truths:

1. ***You're Intrinsic Worth:*** You possess inherent value simply by existing. You were meticulously crafted by the divine, without flaws or errors. Recognise that you are a unique creation, imbued with immeasurable worth.

2. ***Acknowledge Your Gifts:*** Each individual possesses distinct talents and strengths. Seek input from trusted sources to identify your areas of giftedness. Embracing these abilities reinforces your value and highlights your contributions to your family and society.

3. ***Authenticity Breeds Connection:*** Maintaining a facade of perfection can perpetuate misconceptions about your well-being. Instead, cultivate openness and vulnerability with loved ones. Sharing your struggles allows them to offer support and encouragement, reaffirming that you are not alone in your journey.

In moments of self-doubt, remember these truths to counteract feelings of worthlessness. Engage in activities that bring you joy and fulfilment, whether it's cooking, cleaning, reading, or assisting others. By actively pursuing activities you love, you can combat negative emotions and find solace in meaningful pursuits.

I personally navigated through periods of depression by immersing myself in activities I enjoyed, such as reading, writing, and taking leisurely walks in the countryside near my residence in Noak Hill, Essex, UK. By staying active and engaged in my interests, I found respite from my struggles and regained a sense of purpose and fulfilment.

FRIENDS

A friend in need is a friend indeed. I've been incredibly fortunate with the friends I've had. I've always taken care of my friends, and I owe much of my success to the grace of God and the wonderful friendships He has blessed me with. Some of these friendships have lasted for over four decades.

The support of my friends helped me overcome dyslexia. When I was struggling and feeling lost, a friend entered my life and introduced me to a technical college to study automobile engineering. Things were tough initially in college, as I struggled with reading and writing, but a few compassionate individuals befriended me and helped me navigate through my challenges. One friend in particular, Ayo Adetutu, went above and beyond to ensure I was okay both inside and outside of the classroom. However, not all my college peers understood or were sympathetic to my struggles. Some even bullied me, but the presence of supportive friends by my side gave me strength.

I have spoken about my childhood and as now you know that growing up, I faced difficulties at home, especially with my mother. Her hurtful words and rejection deeply affected me – even into my adulthood. So much of what should have been normal in my life was foreign to me; for instance, it wasn't until my 21st birthday celebration, prompted by friends, that I understood the true significance of birthdays. From then on, I embraced the tradition, finding joy in celebrating each year, whether with friends or in solitude.

After completing college, I was among the fortunate few students employed by what was then called UTC Motors, a French motor company. I had my own living quarters and invited friends to stay with me, creating a supportive community away from our families. Life was enjoyable, and although we were often mistaken for troublemakers, eventually we were respected in our neighbourhood for our good character.

My journey took a turn when I left Nigeria on a scholarship to study mechanical engineering. I encountered what one might call "bad company," friends who treated me poorly and belittled me because of my educational background. I continued to help others, even those who mistreated me and found solace and happiness in embracing life's milestones and forging my path forward. Some friendships did turn sour.

Amidst these experiences, I'm grateful for the true friendships I've maintained, particularly with friends like Kay

Oluyemi, Gbenga Odeoyinbo, Duro Lawal, and many others. These friendships have stood the test of time and continue to enrich my life.

I'm thankful for my dear wife, who possesses a keen sense for identifying bad influences among friends. While men may be less discerning in this regard, it's essential to be cautious and selective about the company we keep. Through all the challenges I've faced with friendships, I recognise the value of having companions who share knowledge, provide support, and uplift us during difficult times.

Two things in life are guaranteed, life and death. We all go through times of loss and after my mother passed away, at the age of 120, I mourned for days. I deeply missed her presence. She was a remarkable woman, possessing beauty, intelligence, friendliness, and kindness. Despite giving her more trouble than any of my siblings, her absence left a profound void in my life.

Regardless of their age at the time of passing, the loss of a parent is deeply felt. My mother's departure in 2007 marked a significant event in my life, and even now, many years later, memories of her remain vivid – as though they just happened yesterday.

WEATHERING THE STORM: SMALL VICTORIES

The past few years plunged us into the darkest times of our generation. Life, as we know it, seems shrouded in darkness. Many of us harbour fears, uncertain of how long this will endure. Yet, amidst the shadows, the sun inevitably rises. The dawn breaks, signalling that darkness does not have the final say.

Amidst the chaos of the pandemic, I found myself battling the most challenging period of my life. Hospitalised during Christmas and New Year, uncertainty loomed over my health as my family fervently prayed for my recovery. Meanwhile, I grappled with concerns about their well-being during the festive season. The subsequent months brought further trials as various family members faced health crises, leaving me to juggle caregiving responsibilities alongside my own struggles.

Emerging from the hospital at the year's onset, I faced a cascade of challenges - from health issues to mounting pressure at work. Regardless of the weight of my burdens, I found solace in studying, writing, and engaging in online preaching. However, the months that followed brought fresh turmoil as my wife and niece endured hospitalisations, and we mourned the loss of loved ones.

Just as I glimpsed a glimmer of hope, news of my mother-in-law's cancer spread cast a pall over our family. Her subsequent passing, along with other familial losses, left us reeling. Amidst the grief, however, the arrival of my granddaughter brought a ray of joy, albeit tinged with sorrow for those we had lost.

As the tumultuous year drew to a close, financial struggles persisted, compounded by the lingering effects of COVID-19. Amidst it all I found solace in reconnecting with family in Nigeria and enjoying a brief respite in Paris with my wife and daughter.

With my father-in-law's health declining, we made the decision to bring him into our home, hoping to provide comfort in his time of grief. As we navigate these trials together, I am reminded of the resilience of the human spirit and the enduring power of faith in sustaining us through life's darkest storms.

PIT STOPS

It's time for us to become adept at manoeuvring through the unexpected, recognising that amidst life's surprises, both positive and negative, we must trust God, expecting Him to intervene while leading us forward. We must acknowledge that He never intended for us to lead mundane and predictable lives, regardless of our efforts to establish regular routines. He has called us to embrace a life teeming with joys and sorrows, struggles and triumphs, successes and setbacks, highs and lows. Moreover, He desires for us to anticipate gaining from the unexpected, especially as the world becomes increasingly chaotic and unpredictable.

In our humanity, we may strive to control everything, even God. Yet, we serve a God who refuses to be constrained by us. This is because a significant aspect of the mystery and adventure of following Jesus is placing our trust in Him, regardless of the circumstances surrounding us. It involves keeping our hearts open to Him, so that when the unexpected occurs, He can utilise it for our benefit. It involves allowing Him to leverage the unexpected as a necessary catalyst for our growth, sanctification, and for imparting a fresh perspective on life, for growth and progress are often accompanied by disruption and interruption.

If we could internalise this truth deeply within ourselves, we would experience far less fear in a world that is complex and ever-changing. We could find solace in knowing that while we cannot control the unexpected, God is in control of everything, and thus, we can confidently expect Him to remain faithful to the promises He has made in His Word.

Erma Bombeck, the humorist, once quipped, If life is a bowl of cherries, then what am I doing in the pits? Life isn't always a bed of roses; sometimes, it's filled with challenges.

Jesus himself acknowledged in John 16:33, In this world, you will have trouble. But take heart! I have overcome the world. Along the journey to your dreams, you're bound to encounter a few pits stops. What you do when you find yourself in the pit can determine whether it's just a temporary pause or a prolonged stay.

Consider the story from 1978 of a young man who faced a setback. He was dismissed from his job at a local hardware store. While getting fired can feel like hitting rock bottom, instead of resigning himself to a pit stop, he transformed it into an opportunity. He saw it as a chance to start his own business. Teaming up with a partner, they envisioned opening a hardware store. Their first store opened in 1979, and today they boast over 2000 stores globally. That young man was Bernard Marcus, and the store they founded became known as The Home Depot.

What you make of your time in the pit can either embitter you or empower you, it all boils down to your attitude. Why not choose to view the pit as a classroom and learn some invaluable lessons?

In a Peanuts comic strip, Linus remarks to Charlie Brown, you know, Charlie Brown, they say we learn more from losing than from winning. To which Charlie Brown wryly responds, then that must make me the smartest person in the world. Indeed, setbacks can be disheartening, yet some of life's most profound lessons can only be learned from the pits.

Hebrews 5:8 illuminates that even Jesus, the epitome of perfection, learned obedience through the things that He suffered. This verse underscores the notion that certain lessons can only be grasped through trials and tribulations. While it's not anyone's desire to endure hardship, there's wisdom to be gained in the pit. So, seize the opportunity to turn your pit into a classroom and extract the valuable insights it offers.

What are some lessons you've gleaned from your time in the pit?

The adventure that lies ahead, fraught with unforeseen twists and turns, where the odds may seem stacked against us, is precisely where God intends us to be. Positioned perfectly to walk in faith, anticipating signs, wonders, and miracles, and expecting the supernatural to unfold.

God desires for us to perceive every unexpected occurrence as an opportunity to rely on Jesus and His teachings, to anticipate His goodness throughout the journey. A life lived with such faith is an incredibly potent force, as it generates a momentum of courage and trust that propels us into uncharted territories.

What if we learned to embrace life's unforeseen shocks, stressors, and fluctuations, and then leverage them for our benefit? Perhaps there's a perspective, a paradigm shift, in the way we approach life that needs to occur. Maybe there's a level of trust beyond merely believing that all things work together for our good" (Romans 8:28). Perhaps there's more to it.

Often, when situations deteriorate before they improve, when challenges intensify before they ease, and when darkness looms before light, doubts arise. We question God. We question His purpose. We question His steadfastness. We become discouraged. We may think, Maybe God didn't open that door. Maybe He didn't call me. Perhaps this isn't His will." But when did God promise that life would be easy? When did He guarantee that it would be effortless? One crucial lesson I've learned time and time again is that closed doors do not signify that God isn't making a way. Increased challenges do not imply that God isn't calling.

The presence of a battle doesn't indicate God's absence in the conflict.

Trials don't signify that we're out of God's will. Often, they signify that we're precisely where we should be, doing precisely what we should be doing—fighting the good fight of faith, standing firm, believing. Because He is orchestrating all things for our benefit... and more!

In essence, expectations are the beliefs that arise from a person's thought process when assessing evidence. For instance, observing the eastern sky turn pink may lead us to expect the imminent appearance of the sun. However, our expectations aren't always accurate due to flaws in reasoning and the influence of hope and desire. Sometimes, we set expectations automatically, without conscious effort. When our expectations aren't met, it often leads to disappointment, and we may attribute blame to something or someone who failed to meet our expectations, even if they were unrealistic.

Expectations grounded in human assumptions can lead to problems. For example, when a couple gets married, each brings certain expectations into the relationship. If these expectations aren't met, it can result in hurt feelings, resentment, and conflict. Faulty expectations can create trouble in any relationship where there is mutual dependency, whether it's between parents and children, employers and employees, friends, ministry partners, or teammates. When expectations are unmet, conflict may arise, highlighting the importance of managing expectations effectively.

Frequently, our expectations are shaped by our upbringing, family dynamics, or personal inclinations. For instance, if you were raised in a household where conflict resolution involved shouting and confrontation, you might anticipate others to react similarly if they have an issue with you. Conversely, someone who prefers to address problems calmly may struggle to convey their hurt feelings, since they're not yelling, you might assume the issue isn't serious, inadvertently perpetuating behaviours that upsets them.

Fear does not originate from God, nor is it more potent than God. However, God foresaw that fear would attempt to steal our peace repeatedly throughout our lives. Thus, in His boundless mercy and faithfulness, God equipped us with three offensive weapons to combat fear: For God has not given us a spirit of fear, but of power and of love and of a sound mind" (2 Timothy 1:7, NKJV).

This verse unequivocally identifies fear as a spiritual force contrary to God's nature. Therefore, whenever fear attempts to grip us, it's the enemy's strategy to instil terror and undermine our trust in God. However, the spirit of fear cannot withstand the indwelling Spirit of God, who empowers us with strength, love, and clarity of mind. We can draw upon His presence, relying on His peace amidst fear and anxiety, knowing that He who resides within us is greater than any opposition we face.

When we lean on the Holy Spirit, we can take solace in knowing that we're not fighting alone. Our battle is fought in God's power, not by fixating on fear and attempting to conquer it in our own strength, but by trusting in God and embracing the power, love, and clarity of mind He has bestowed upon us.

I've discovered that the more I place my trust in my heavenly Father, the more fear diminishes in my heart and mind. By focusing on God more than on unexpected circumstances, He becomes paramount in my thoughts and emotions, resulting in peace.

God's Word assures us that the path He has set before us ascends, not descends. However, to stay on this upward trajectory mentally, emotionally, and physically, we must magnify Him in our lives.

God desires us to trust Him rather than worry, regardless of what the future holds. Trusting God is not a one-time event but an ongoing process, a daily, hourly, sometimes minute-by-minute journey that fosters consistent growth. Through this process, we face trials, experience peace, only to encounter unexpected challenges again. However, with each cycle, we grow stronger and more resilient.

During moments of discouragement, God encourages us to lean on Him: "I have told you these things, so that in me you may have peace. In this world you will have trouble. But take heart! I have overcome the world" (John 16:33). In this verse, "trouble" denotes being crushed or overwhelmed by unsolved problems. We're urged to persevere in faith, trusting that God will bring us through no matter the challenge.

When we choose to anticipate instead of worry, we can live with hearts filled with hope. By expecting the best rather than the worst, we can lead lives imbued with faith.

Imagine the freedom we'd experience if we genuinely believed that trust is the antidote to fear in every situation. Picture growing to a point where trusting God is our instinctive response. "Trust in the Lord with all your heart and lean not on your own understanding; in all your ways submit to him, and he will make your paths straight" (Proverbs 3:5-6).

It's time for us to adopt this approach to life. I've learned that every experience—both expected and unexpected—is purposeful in God's plan. He uses these experiences to shape and propel us toward our future. God desires us to reach a level of faith where we eagerly anticipate the blessings, He has in store for us as we continue to trust Him, regardless of our circumstances. This transformation is integral to becoming more like Christ.

Even when faced with imminent death on the cross, Jesus looked beyond His immediate suffering, considering the impact of His present circumstances on our future. He demonstrated how to live free from fear amidst the unexpected. The apostle Peter later drew upon Christ's example, urging believers not to be surprised by fiery trials but to rejoice, knowing that these trials produce endurance and ultimately lead to joy (1 Peter 4:12–13 NKJV).

Let's not allow fear to condition us to expect the worst. Instead, let's courageously face each new event, trusting that God will work wonders in our lives. Let's remember that He will never abandon us.

SEVENTY

When my friend first suggested I write my autobiography, I wasn't excited. However, after engaging in deep conversations with my friend about my life experiences, I began to see the value in such a project. Reflecting on my journey, I realised that this was something I should pursue. Years before, I had enrolled in a Creative Writing course at UCL (University of Central London), but I soon realised it wasn't the right fit as it focused more on journalism than creative writing, prompting me to drop out halfway through the first year.

Despite this setback, my family, friends, and mentors encouraged me to document my life story for future generations, especially those close to me. Throughout my life, I've encountered individuals whom I believe were sent by God to support me during both the highs and lows. Some came with genuine intentions to help, while others sought to exploit or undermine what I had built. Dealing with such people only strengthened my resolve and motivated me to prove them wrong, ultimately propelling me closer to my destiny.

Each challenge I faced and overcame not only helped me grow but also presented opportunities to solve problems for others.

I always maintained a vision for a better tomorrow, keeping my gaze fixed on the distant horizon. This book delves into the journey of how I learned to navigate life's hurdles, recognising that I have been living on the edge of tomorrow in both my professional and family life. I continue to dream big, firmly believing that one day, everything will fall into place.

My journey began on October 1st, 1979, and here I am over forty years later, still reflecting on the twists and turns. Over 36 years of marriage, my love for my wife remains as strong as the day we met. I pray for the chance to rekindle the passion of our early years.

Blessed with five children and a wonderful wife, my life has taken me from Romania to France, the United States, and finally the United Kingdom. Despite humble beginnings in a remote part of Nigeria, where I didn't learn to read and write until I was 18, I've faced many challenges. Bullies, humiliation, and academic struggles marked my early years, but I've been fortunate to have a loving family and good health.

Friendship has been both a blessing and a challenge. While some friends betrayed me, others remained steadfast. I've learned the value of loyalty and trust over the years.

My journey led me to London, where I met my wife. We married when she was 21, and we were blessed with five children, including a granddaughter in 2021.

Turning sixty has filled me with immense gratitude towards God. While I may not have everything I desired in life, I've come to realise that I have everything I truly need.

Following the closure of my business, which had been running for twenty-six years, due to my wife's illness and the serious sickness of two of my children, as well as financial losses, I made the difficult decision to shut down the business and focus on my family. In the midst of all of this, I persisted in pursuing my passion for writing, and in 2011, I successfully published my first book. My motto became: never give up on your dreams. Writing a book had been a long-held vision of mine, and though it took time to materialise, I persevered. During this period, I also ventured into buying and selling items on eBay, including cars, to supplement my income, albeit at a slow pace. Three years later, I began actively searching for employment. The opportunity arose during the 2012 Olympics, where I worked briefly. Following the Olympics, I underwent security training, obtained my SIA license, CCTV certification, NVQ Level 2, and First Aid training. Subsequently, I embarked on a job hunt, which culminated in securing my first job in 2015.

With the ongoing pressures at home, I continue to persevere, firmly believing that it's not over until God decrees it so. The road to success has been fraught with obstacles. For individuals facing circumstances similar to mine, with seemingly no light at the end of the tunnel, I urge them to keep pushing forward and never lose hope. Seeking employment at the age of seventy is no easy feat. When I share news of my employment with friends and family, it often comes as a surprise.

In such circumstances, the security sector is often the most accessible avenue for employment after obtaining relevant training, especially for older individuals amidst a competitive job market where many young graduates struggle to find work. I remained steadfast, placing my trust in God and prioritising my physical fitness to provide for my family.

One of the most challenging aspects of my situation is the feeling of loneliness, exacerbated by age and health issues such as high blood pressure, diabetes, and back pain. In today's world, most people are preoccupied with their own lives, leaving little time for social interaction. There was a lack of external support, but I chose to focus on embracing each new day with optimism. Life's journey resembles a train voyage, with passengers embarking and disembarking at various stations until reaching the final destination. Along the way, many individuals seek happiness through material wealth, resorting to drastic measures such as robbery, fraud, or even harming loved ones. However, the truth is that money alone cannot guarantee happiness.

A LONG-LASTING MARRIAGE

In the intricate tapestry of marriage, communication stands as the linchpin. My journey with Victoria, my wife of over three decades, commenced with a chance encounter at a friend's residence in Battersea, London. Following our initial meeting, months passed before we reunited, our bond gradually blossoming into something profound. Our marriage weathered its fair share of storms, yet fortified by divine grace, we navigated through the rough patches. Despite not always having everything we desired, we cherished the intangible treasures money cannot buy: our five beautiful children, a roof over our heads, and sustenance on our table. Our commitment to honesty and mutual trust served as the bedrock of our union, complemented by a swift resolution of conflicts and the unwavering support of our families.

Reflecting on our journey, encompassing the highs of courtship and the challenges of parenthood and entrepreneurship, I feel an overwhelming sense of pride. Our shared experiences have forged an unbreakable bond, propelling us towards growth and maturity as individuals and as partners. Marriage, I've come to realise, transcends mere companionship; it's a testament to two flawed yet resilient souls striving to understand and uplift each other. Even with the unpredictability of life's twists and turns, sustained communication and unwavering commitment have been our guiding lights, illuminating the path forward through every trial and triumph.

Admittedly, I haven't always been the best listener in my marriage. Surprisingly, I find myself more attentive at work than I am at home, and whilst making improvements over the years, I still have a long way to go. Listening can be challenging, especially for someone as prideful as myself. My wife and I, despite enjoying many activities together, are individuals with strong opinions, making understanding each other crucial. I've come to realise that seeking to understand my spouse's perspective before seeking to be understood greatly benefits our marriage. Understanding doesn't necessarily mean agreeing with everything my spouse says, but rather grasping their viewpoint to move forward together in unity. Unfortunately, spouses sometimes overlook this vital aspect.

Here's an example of a scenario in our household where I failed to understand my wife's perspective: Recently, she asked me to clear some beds in our backyard for an upcoming neighbourhood party. However, I responded brusquely, citing other tasks I needed to complete first. In hindsight, my tone was disrespectful, and I failed to acknowledge her efforts in managing household chores and childcare. Neither of us was solely at fault for the issue; we both neglected to understand each other's priorities and timeframes. Over the years, we've learned the importance of active listening and have adopted some uncommon yet effective strategies to enhance our communication:

1. STOP: Pause what you're doing and give your full attention to your partner.

2. EYE CONTACT: Maintain eye contact to show attentiveness and avoid distractions.

3. LISTEN WITH YOUR EARS, NOT YOUR MOUTH: Refrain from interjecting or offering advice; simply listen.

4. REPHRASE OR REPEAT: Reflect back what your partner said to ensure understanding.

5. DOUBLE CHECK: Clarify any ambiguous points to prevent misunderstandings.

6. USE EMPATHY: Strive to comprehend your spouse's perspective, even if it's challenging, and refrain from immediately offering solutions.

This week, I challenged myself to be quick to listen and slow to anger in my interactions with my spouse. I'll actively seek feedback on how I can become a better listener and implement their suggestions. In marriage, there are moments of joy and disappointment, but effective communication remains the key to navigating through them together.

MY CHILDREN

I have five of the most wonderful children one could ever wish for. They are delightful, beautiful souls. My journey into parenthood began at the age of 31 with the arrival of my firstborn, Richard, on December 31, 1986. It was during our journey home from a New Year's Eve prayer meeting that we first noticed his seizures. As a young couple, we were naive and didn't understand how a child so young could develop such a serious condition.

Richard's seizures persisted for eight years, leaving a lasting impact on him. Thankfully, our second child, Sam, has been healthy and has never faced any medical issues. Comfort, our third child, entered the world prematurely, six weeks ahead of schedule. Although she initially seemed fine, she began experiencing epileptic fits at the age of eight, which have continued to affect her significantly. Even at the age of 26, she was still struggling with the aftermath of the damage to her brain.

Michael, our fourth child, was born without any complications, while Joy, the youngest, arrived ten days premature. During her birth, she stopped taking in food, prompting the doctors to induce her. Although she was physically okay at birth, she later developed dyslexia and struggles with understanding numbers and money.

Three of my children were born with a hole in the heart, with two requiring surgical intervention while one was fortunate enough to have the hole close on its own.

Through it all we never allowed the challenges to overshadow our lives. We continued to live as normally as possible, though it was undeniably difficult. Some members of our family blamed us for not being good enough as parents, and they held us responsible for the conditions our children experienced. My wife also faced unwarranted criticism from close quarters, with people attributing our children's conditions to familial sins and inadequate prayers.

I consider myself blessed and resilient, fuelled by the love and encouragement of my children. My children's presence always brings me immense joy, and I refuse to see their disabilities as limitations but rather as an opportunity to embrace life from a different perspective.

No one is flawless, and criticism comes regardless of whether we do things right or wrong. This never bothered me much until my wife's car accident began to take its toll on her health. As she underwent three operations and battled with DVT, I assumed the role of caretaker for her and our five children, all while managing our household and running our business.

How I managed to juggle everything remains a mystery to me, but I credit it all to the grace of God. Surviving such trials is only possible through His divine intervention. If you find yourself in a similar situation, my advice to you is simple: never give up.

In my youth, I was stubborn and abhorred injustice. I valued fairness, refused to give up easily, and possessed a deep love for people. I detested being underestimated and would go to great lengths to assist others. I am a hard-working individual who despises begging or borrowing.

I never truly understood love until I met my first girlfriend, Shade. We dated for twelve and a half years, but as you know, things didn't work out between us. However, I believe that everything happens for a reason as I went on to meet and marry a woman that exceeded my expectations.

My wife loves me unconditionally and is willing to sacrifice anything for my success. She is the love of my life, and our bond remains as strong as it was when we first met in 1984, in Battersea, Southeast London. Though we have our differences, the secret to our enduring marriage lies in communication, forgiveness, and praying together each night and day. For those who don't believe in prayer, it may be challenging to grasp its significance, but for us, it has been an essential pillar of our relationship.

GUIDING WITH GRACE: PARENTAL SUPPORT AND ENCOURAGEMENT

Raising five remarkable children has been an enlightening journey for me. Among the most impactful lessons I've learned is the profound influence of written communication, particularly in the form of letters, to inspire and uplift my children.

Communicating with your children verbally is one thing, but putting your feelings into writing and sharing the vision you hold for their lives serves as a tangible testament to your care and affection. In today's era of text messages, handwritten letters hold a special rarity. If you take the time to jot down your thoughts, your children will regard them with earnestness, having something tangible to hold onto and revisit time and again. You may very well create a cherished keepsake that they will treasure for years to come.

If you feel that you lack the flair for writing, please don't allow that to deter you. Feel free to draw inspiration from others or to incorporate quotes from poetry or verses from relevant songs. Let nothing hinder you from penning what could potentially be the most significant letter of your life! Find a quiet space and begin by jotting down bullet points or the initial thoughts that come to mind. Craft multiple drafts if necessary, and if it puts you at ease, seek the feedback of a trusted friend or, if you prefer, even a complete stranger.

So, what should your letter encompass? Here are a few suggestions to help you get started:

1. ***Express your love unequivocally:*** This need not be elaborate or poetic, though it certainly can be. Regardless of how you phrase it, your children should walk away from the letter knowing beyond doubt that you love them. Even the simple words "I love you," written on a line by themselves, suffice. But it is crucial to convey this message unmistakably in some form or another. Today's teenagers often express a deep longing to feel loved above all else. And frankly, if they harbour any doubts about your love for them, then regardless of your other efforts, you have fallen short.

2. ***Share your vision for their future:*** If you have not already done so then you should craft a vision statement for your family. Write about who you are as a family and where you are going, where do you plan to be ten years from now and how things will look? You can then incorporate this into your letter. A family that holds a unified vision is a strong family, destined for greatness.

3. Offer a prayer for them: Let your children know what you pray about concerning them. It is a blessing for them to know that you pray for them and also beneficial for them to have an understanding of what you pray and comprehend the content of your petitions. Your prayers communicate love, hope and faith.

Whilst we are on the subject of supporting and encouraging your children, remember, don't turn your home into a "NO Zone." I've participated in numerous radio interviews addressing the imperative of safeguarding our homes and families from the encroaching influences of a debased culture. Often, a well-meaning caller will assert, "I agree that the culture is corrupt, so I've removed all the TVs, banned the Internet from my house, and prohibited my kids from having cell phones." Unfortunately, these parents have misidentified technology and hardware as the problem. The issue isn't the technology itself but rather how we employ it and allow others to misuse it within our homes. Rather than wholesale prohibition, we should harness the benefits of technology while filtering out the negative aspects. We should establish boundaries without completely severing access.

You can and should cultivate a relaxed atmosphere in your home, but you cannot afford to let your guard down. Establish firm guidelines without turning your household into a boot camp. How you articulate and instil your standards is just as crucial in safeguarding your children as the rules and precautions you implement for your family's well-being. Consider the wisdom shared by Shannon, a woman who offers guidance on saying both yes and no to younger children:

"I strive to say yes as often as possible, even if it means saying, 'Yes, we can do that tomorrow,' or 'Yes, you may have five raisins instead of the three hundred you want.' And when I must say no, I endeavour to maintain a cheerful tone and a loving demeanour. After all, the denial pertains to the object in question, not to the child. 'No, you may not have another popsicle right now.' Nope. Nope. Nope. Often, my little ones will smile in response. And if they persist, I remain cheerful and say, 'Nope! But we can read a story, and if you're hungry, you can have a snack.' And if they continue to inquire, I'll say, 'What's the answer to that question?' I reserve the stern countenance for instances of defiance, cruelty to others, or perilous behaviour.

When issuing directives and setting boundaries, I strive to frame them in a positive light as often as possible. For instance, 'Clean up the spill,' is preferable too 'Don't spill.' And 'Use your indoor voice, please,' is more constructive than 'Don't whine!'"

Shannon's advice can be applied to teenagers as well. "Yes, you may invite friends over, provided you complete your homework first." "Yes, you may go to the movies once you've helped me tidy up." It's not about saying yes to everything but rather about shifting your focus so the glass is seen as half full rather than half empty whilst you still implement the necessary boundaries needed for their safety, development and growth.

You should seek to be a friendly parent and not just a friend. This can be achieved through the following steps:

Establish Clear Boundaries: Define specific boundaries, such as non-homework computer time, to avoid ambiguity. Providing vague warnings like "Don't stay on there too long" leads to confusion. Instead, clearly state limits, such as "You're allowed X minutes online," and adhere to them consistently. This principle applies to all areas of life; ensure your expectations are communicated as clearly as possible.

Enforce Rules: Rules are not negative; they are there for your benefit and your children. Rules safeguard and protect but rules without enforcement are ineffective and lack meaning. Repeatedly admonishing children without consequences only fosters disrespect for authority. It's better to remain silent than to continually issue warnings that go unheeded. Enforcement of rules is essential to instilling discipline and respect.

Avoid Pleading: Rather than pleading with your children to behave, make it unequivocal that obedience is expected. Despite the negative connotations of obedience in today's culture, it is crucial for your children's success in life. Teaching them to obey prepares them for responsibilities at school and in the workplace.

Prioritise Character Development: Character is primarily concerned with the development of your child's identity rather than solely their actions; what your children do reflects who they are. Prioritise the cultivation of your children's character and equip them for achievement instead of chasing popularity. Parenting demands dedication, establishing and upholding standards out of love rather than seeking validation.

Discipline Calmly: Discipline should never be administered in anger. This is something that may take time and practice. If you can learn to always take time to cool off before addressing misbehaviour, you will ensure punishments are just and not merely reactionary. Delay disciplinary discussions if necessary and follow through later once you are calmer and able to think rationally rather than emotionally.

It's widely understood that leading by example carries greater weight, as children tend to emulate our actions more than they heed our words. You must lead by example because your children will do as you do.

Align Actions with Words: Actions speak louder than words; children observe and emulate parental behaviour. If your actions contradict your words, children will disregard the latter. Maintain consistency between your words and deeds to set a positive example.

Children Learn by Observation: Children learn from observing their parents' interactions and reactions. They emulate behaviours they witness, whether positive or negative. Modelling good behaviour, such as listening attentively and speaking respectfully, positively influences children's conduct.

Strive for Consistency: Children learn from patterns in parental behaviour. Aim to set consistent, positive examples for them to emulate, recognising that occasional mistakes are inevitable. Your behaviour shapes their perceptions and habits.

Be a Role Model in a Culture of Immaturity: In a society that often glorifies childish behaviour, strive to exemplify maturity and self-control. Whilst media influences celebrate impulsivity and immaturity, you must maintain integrity and honour in your conduct. Children look to you for guidance, even when you're unaware.

Parents, it's crucial to take your parental responsibility seriously. Acknowledge the significant impact you wield over your children and willingly accept the duty to exemplify positive behaviour. Make a firm commitment to demonstrate actions worth emulating.

EFFORT, OWNERSHIP AND FULFILLMENT

I would like to tell you a short story about two young girls who each coveted an American Girl doll.

Amy desired Samantha for her luscious brown curls and fashionable early-twentieth-century attire. Meanwhile, Karina had her heart set on Felicity, drawn to her charming hats and frilly dresses. Both girls, in fourth grade, approached their mothers with requests for the dolls they admired.

Amy's parents, despite their ability to afford multiple dolls, opted to instil a sense of ownership and responsibility in their daughter. They informed Amy that she would need to devise a method to earn the doll of her choice. After thoughtful consideration, they explained to her that her diligent behaviour, consistent completion of chores and homework, warranted the opportunity to earn the doll.

They presented Amy with a challenge: memorise and recite every state capital in the country, and Samantha would be hers. They emphasised that such a prized possession as Samantha required effort and dedication. Interestingly, each American Girl doll is accompanied by a series of books detailing her unique story. In Samantha's tale, she, too, is tasked by her grandmother to earn her desired doll through diligence in piano lessons.

Motivated by Samantha's fictional journey, Amy eagerly committed herself to memorising the state capitals. Upon successfully reciting them, her parents fulfilled their promise, presenting her with the cherished doll. Amy cherished Samantha, appreciating the doll as a product of her hard work and determination.

In contrast, when Karina expressed her desire for Felicity, her mother promptly purchased the doll without requiring any effort on Karina's part. However, Karina quickly grew bored with Felicity and soon requested another doll, Molly. Even with initial resistance from her mother, Karina's persistence led to the acquisition of multiple dolls over time.

Unlike Amy, Karina acquired her dolls effortlessly, yet she remained unsatisfied, constantly seeking more. Amy, on the other hand, derived profound satisfaction from earning her doll through dedication and perseverance.

This tale illustrates a fundamental truth: humans find greater fulfilment when they know they have earned their possessions. Instilling this sense of satisfaction through hard work and effort is a valuable lesson that should be imparted to children early in life.

The story of Amy and Karina highlights the importance of instilling a sense of ownership and responsibility in your children. Amy's journey, where she earned her desired doll through hard work and diligence, resulted in deep satisfaction and appreciation for her possession. In contrast, Karina's effortless acquisition of dolls left her unsatisfied and constantly seeking more. This teaches us that true fulfilment comes from earning our possessions through dedication and perseverance rather than having them handed to us. As parents and educators, we should prioritise teaching children the value of hard work and the satisfaction that comes from earning their belongings. This lesson not only fosters a sense of responsibility but also sets the foundation for a fulfilling and successful life.

A GOOD FATHER

A responsible father is someone who prioritises keeping his family together at all costs, standing by them through thick and thin. There are moments in life when we feel tempted to throw in the towel, to seek solace elsewhere or in someone we perceive as better or more attractive. I've experienced such moments myself, where I felt disillusioned and contemplated giving up, seeking fulfilment elsewhere. However, I made a vow before I got married that I would never divorce or remarry, and I'm grateful that I've been able to keep that promise.

Growing up in a polygamous environment, where everyone in the village had multiple wives, I came to understand the rationale behind it - more wives meant more children and more help on the farm. However, as I ventured beyond the village and into the bustling city of

Lagos, I realised that such practices weren't as applicable in urban settings.

My upbringing was marked by instability, shuffled between relatives without the love and care of both parents. This shaped my perspective on parenting and instilled in me a determination to provide my children with a better upbringing. Despite lacking a formal education due to my disability, I worked tirelessly to ensure my children received the best education and that my family was well taken care of. And to a large extent, I succeeded. Today, I have no regrets. I am blessed with a loving wife and children who appreciate my efforts. I aspire for my children to lead better lives than mine, as I've faced many challenges and hardships along the way.

Every human has a father, but not all experience the presence of a good dad. However, irrespective of our earthly father's role, we all have a heavenly Father who loves and cares for us deeply. Through Christ, we are adopted as sons and daughters, blessed with a Father who provides, guides, and loves us unconditionally. His love surpasses anything we could ever imagine, and his greatest desire is for us to know that we are cherished and beloved.

EMPOWERING FATHERS: BUILDING STRONG BONDS WITH SONS

Being a dad to sons is an incredibly rewarding journey, yet it comes with significant responsibilities. The alarming fatherhood crisis prevailing in our society today, evident in statistics showcasing the detrimental effects of fatherlessness on juvenile court systems, prisons, and schools, necessitates action. Instead of idly standing by, it's time for fathers to step up and make a positive impact.

For those already excelling in fatherhood, keep up the fantastic work! However, if you find yourself drifting without a solid plan for raising your son, this concise read aims to inspire you to elevate your parenting game.

Fathering sons demands earnest commitment from dedicated men. Here are three crucial messages every son should hear or witness from his father:

1. You Are Loved: Every son deserves to hear expressions of love from his father. Affirmation from a father holds immense significance, influencing key relationships throughout life. Therefore, it's vital to verbalise your love for your son. Take a moment, kneel down to his level, lock eyes, and sincerely convey, "Son, I love you." Accompany this with a warm embrace, witnessing the profound impact it has on your son's confidence.

2. I'm Proud of You: Offering periodic affirmation of pride to your son is essential. Many men seek approval in various areas, often yearning for validation from their fathers. Remind your son of his worthiness and your unwavering support. Recall the biblical example of God affirming His Son, Jesus, to comprehend the power of approval. Look your son in the eyes and affirm, "Son, I'm proud of you," reinforcing his sense of value and acceptance.

While the Bible may not directly address single mothers, its teachings on God's compassion and support extend to all individuals, regardless of their familial status. Whether single, married, widowed, or divorced, God offers solace and assistance to those in need. He urges repentance, fostering a relationship founded on trust and reliance on Him. For single mothers burdened with numerous responsibilities, prioritising time for prayer and scripture reading can provide strength and solace. Despite the challenges of balancing work, childcare, and household duties, dedicating moments to commune with God yields immeasurable benefits. Through faith and prayer, single mothers can find comfort in God's promises and experience His unwavering support amidst life's trials.

In conclusion, God's message to single mothers echoes His divine love and provision for all. By embracing repentance, fostering communication with God, and trusting in His guidance, single mothers can find hope and strength in His promises. As they navigate life's trials, they can rest assured in the eternal blessings awaiting those who love and trust in Him. Last month, my beloved sister-in-law passed away, leaving a profound void in our family. Her legacy of love, care, and commitment to education serves as a poignant reminder of the impact individuals can have on others' lives. No matter the unexpected problems she faced, her unwavering dedication to nurturing and educating others endures as a beacon of inspiration for us all.

FAMILY BONDING

Ensuring balance in our lives, especially within our families, is essential for nurturing our mental, emotional, and spiritual health. Reflecting on our own journey, my family and I have successfully attained this balance. It took us some time to get there and I'm eager to share some insights on what worked for us, believing they can greatly benefit you when applied in your own life.

Recognising the importance of maintaining a balanced lifestyle, especially for our mental and emotional well-being, is paramount. According to a study conducted at UCLA, finding equilibrium in our busy family schedules is essential.

So how can we reintroduce balance into our hectic family lives? It starts with deliberately incorporating downtime—perhaps even scheduling it. Take a leisurely walk together, opting for a relaxed pace over a hurried one. Engage in a game as a family, preferably a board or card game that encourages interaction around the table.

Moreover, understand that not every activity needs to involve the entire family. Spend quality time with individual children, taking walks or playing games on a rotating basis. Over time, this approach fosters genuine conversations with those closest to us. And don't forget your spouse; regular date nights can significantly strengthen marital bonds.

Gathering for dinner as a family, away from distractions like television, holds immense value. The opportunity to share stories, address concerns, or simply share laughter over a meal is incomparable.

This restoration of balance extends to our spiritual well-being as well. Amid our packed schedules, it's easy to neglect church attendance and daily prayer. However, slowing down is crucial for truly connecting with our faith and hearing the voice of God. While formal retreats are beneficial, the daily "mini retreats" spent in prayer and reflection are equally important.

If you're feeling overwhelmed by your family's schedule, take a step back and assess how time is allocated. Have an open discussion with your family about streamlining extracurricular activities to make room for meaningful family time. Consider implementing a limit on the number of activities each child can participate in per school year, teaching them valuable lessons in prioritisation and time management.

Ultimately, prioritising quality time with our families is about more than creating pleasant memories—it's about nurturing our children to rise above societal pressures and fulfil their God-given potential.

Mother's and Father's, your roles are irreplaceable. While society may not always acknowledge it, your influence on your children's lives is undeniable. Seize the opportunity to cherish their formative years and shape their future, for time passes swiftly. Invest not only in material things for your family but also in the priceless gift of yourself. The returns will far exceed your expectations.

PRAY TOGETHER STAY TOGETHER

The phrase "A family that prays together stays together" resonates deeply with me, as it captures the profound truth that prayer serves as a unifying force within families. It's undeniable that my wife and I have experienced true healing and restoration, all thanks to the grace of almighty God. The scriptures have been my ally, helping me navigate through life's challenges and emerge victorious.

Family holds immense significance to me, especially my children, and I deeply cherish the relationships with those around me. I find joy in the company of others, yet at times, my kindness has been misconstrued as weakness by some relatives and friends. However, I remain resolute in my kindness, understanding that it is a strength, not a weakness. Despite facing numerous setbacks in business, I refuse to apologise for my failures. Instead, I view them as opportunities for growth and resilience. Every failure serves as a steppingstone towards eventual success, and I firmly believe that as long as God permits, it's never too late to turn the tide.

I come from a remarkable family characterised by hard work and boundless love for one another. Even with our modest means, the bond among my siblings remains unbreakable. Recently, I had the opportunity to reunite with my family, and it was a heartwarming experience. Though some of our loved ones have passed away, our gatherings serve as a poignant reminder of the importance of familial connection. I am committed to visiting my family at least once or twice every year, regardless of financial constraints, as their love and support are priceless.

The joy I derive from spending time with my family is immeasurable, and I deeply miss those who are no longer with us. Material wealth pales in comparison to the irreplaceable bond shared with family, and I urge everyone to cherish their loved ones while they are still alive.

WORKING SMART

Many of us put in tremendous effort, working tirelessly day in and day out. However, as a young man freshly arrived in London from Nigeria, I faced immense hardships. There were no fellow countrymen to offer guidance or advice, leaving us feeling adrift like ships without a captain in the vast sea. We relied on trial and error, navigating through life's obstacles with limited resources. Some fortunate individuals had the support of wealthy families to ease their path, while others, like me, had to rely solely on hard work to carve out a future.

I am among those who lacked external support but persevered through sheer determination to reach where I am today. This journey has also instilled in me the importance of preparing my children for the realities of life. Even if I cannot leave them material wealth, I aim to impart invaluable life lessons and skills that will empower them to weather life's storms and thrive independently. It is crucial to equip them with the knowledge and confidence to navigate the obstacles of both the workplace and personal relationships.

In today's world, where technology dominates every aspect of our lives, advancements such as DNA manipulation are reshaping our understanding of human biology and healthcare. The prospect of selecting the traits of our future offspring, including their gender, physical attributes, and even lifespan, is becoming increasingly feasible. The convergence of human biology and technology may lead to revolutionary medical treatments, offering unprecedented control over our health and longevity.

As we embrace these advancements, it's essential to recognise the potential pitfalls of excessive reliance on technology and medication. Our increasingly sedentary lifestyles and over-reliance on smartphones highlight the need to strike a balance between technological innovation and personal well-being. While the future may hold remarkable possibilities, we must remain mindful of the importance of human connection, physical activity, and mental health in leading fulfilling lives.

MANAGING TIME

A friend shared with me her time management strategy, which has proven successful for her. She diligently documents her daily tasks each night, as well as outlines her weekly, monthly, and even yearly activities in a diary. Inspired by her approach, I immediately adopted this practice, finding it immensely helpful in organising my schedule and planning ahead. She emphasised the importance of having a vision for the future, remarking that without proactive planning, others may dictate how our time is spent. She provided an example of how succumbing to impromptu invitations often leads to regret, a scenario I could relate to from personal experience. By mastering time management, she asserted, one can accomplish more in a day than in an entire week.

In the past, I lived with a constant sense of urgency, always rushing to complete tasks and fearing there were never enough hours in the day. However, I eventually realised that time is not a finite resource to be hoarded or squandered; it is a dimension of our experiences. By reframing my perspective on time, I discovered that I could escape the cycle of perpetual busyness and reclaim control over my schedule. Instead of treating time as a commodity to be traded or lost, I learned to leverage it as a tool for productivity and fulfilment. No longer enslaved by the clock, I found myself feeling one step ahead rather than constantly lagging behind. Mundane tasks became more manageable, while moments of leisure felt more abundant.

Becoming time-rich doesn't necessarily mean working longer hours; it's about working smarter and with greater efficiency. Identifying and eliminating time thieves—anything that hinders productivity or induces stress—became a key aspect of my time management strategy. By reclaiming control over my schedule and prioritising tasks effectively, I discovered newfound freedom and satisfaction in my daily routine.

Effective Meeting Participation: Some meetings are unnecessary. Before attending, ask yourself if your presence is indispensable and if the meeting itself is essential. If the answer to both questions is yes, then attend; otherwise, find a polite excuse to skip it. Express that you're mindful of not overcrowding the room. Whenever possible, question the purpose of the meeting. If a meeting is unavoidable, ensure clarity regarding its purpose and assign responsibility for executing any action points. If there's no agenda, request one. If responsibilities are unclear, address them while everyone is present. It's been said that without a clear plan for the day, others will engage you with their own agendas.

Structuring My Day: Structuring my day has been instrumental in overcoming depression, a condition I struggled with for years without realising it. It wasn't until a spiritual leader visited London for a conference and shared his own battle with depression that I understood its significance in my life. During that time, I avoided public places and even attending church, even as a pastor with a sizeable congregation. However, preparing my messages and delving into scripture provided solace. Now that I've identified my struggle with depression, I actively work to overcome it. I structure my days meticulously, planning ahead and listing tasks in advance. Engaging in activities like walking or jogging helps me both physically and mentally. Additionally, my job, which involves long hours standing, contributes to my overall well-being.

Establishing Routine and Habits: Routine and habits offer structure, guiding us from one activity to the next and reducing decision-making stress. Setting specific goals and deadlines boosts confidence and spreads pressure evenly.

Setting Deadlines: Deadlines serve as motivators, ensuring tasks are completed efficiently. While they can be stressful, realistic deadlines promote productivity. It's crucial to strike a balance that maintains efficiency without overwhelming oneself.

Keeping a Diary for a Week: Maintaining a diary allows for reflection on daily activities and emotions. This insight enables adjustments to one's routine, ensuring a healthy balance between productivity and relaxation. Surrounding oneself with positivity and avoiding negative influences further contributes to overall well-being.

. . .

MY MOTHER

My mother's departure left behind a legacy of 252 grandchildren and great-grandchildren spanning four generations. She graced our lives for 120 remarkable years, embodying love, care, and an unwavering sense of honesty. Her strict yet forthright demeanour endeared her to all who knew her, and her passing marked the end of an era. I had a deep desire to attend her funeral however, circumstances prevented me from doing so as my daughter had undergone heart surgery mere weeks before. Our family's focus shifted to supporting her recovery at Great Ormond Street Hospital in London, forcing us to cancel our planned journey.

My mother was a visionary, one of the contemporary matriarchs of our faith. She achieved remarkable feats in her lifetime. Her vision profoundly influenced my journey. To me, she embodied greatness! Yet, I am struck by her reflections on her path. When people inquire what she would alter if given the chance to start anew, she would always respond, "I'd dream bigger! I'd take greater risks. Because every dream I've dared to embrace has materialised. I should have aimed higher!"

DREAM AGAIN

The iPhone stands as a remarkable invention—a manifestation of someone's dream. It serves as a navigation tool, a camera, an entertainment hub, and more. Yet, if you trace its origins, you'll find a store that sold it, a shipping point, a manufacturing plant, and individuals who conceptualised its design. Ultimately, the iPhone originated from someone's imagination.

Every great achievement begins with a dream. Every innovation, every architectural marvel, every masterpiece, every literary work, every cinematic creation—they all originate from a dream.

Renowned filmmaker George Lucas once remarked, "You cannot do it unless you imagine it." Perhaps you already harbour a dream within you. Or maybe you once had a dream that was shattered. The encouraging truth is that God can reignite your imagination.

Repeat this word aloud: "IMAGINE." Say it once more. Now, close your eyes and envision the back of your eyelids as a movie screen, with God directing a film about the remainder of your life. Come on! Engage in this exercise. What do you see? Imagine!

Ephesians 3:20 delivers uplifting news: "God can do infinitely more than we can ask or imagine."

What is beginning to stir within you? Perhaps it's the dream of launching a new business venture. Maybe it's the aspiration to pursue higher education. It could be the desire to pen a book, achieve better health, or find companionship in marriage. Understand that before a dream materialises externally, it must first take shape within.

Walt Disney harboured a vision to establish a theme park in Florida. He acquired the land and drafted plans, yet he passed away from cancer before witnessing it's completion. When the park finally opened in 1971, five years after his demise, someone lamented, "It's a shame Walt didn't live to see this." However, the Disney Creative Director countered, "He did see it." He had visualised it in his heart, and what resided within him came to fruition, transcending his lifetime.

There are dreams that God desires to implant in your heart—dreams so profound that they can outlast you.

What dream is stirring within you?

Henry Ford once emphasised, "Before everything else, getting ready is the secret of success."

When you receive a God-sized dream, readiness becomes paramount. Opportunities don't always present themselves with open windows, but when they do, being prepared to seize them propels you closer to your dream.

Can you recall a moment in your life when an opportunity arose, and you seized it? Alternatively, perhaps you remember a time when you hesitated to act on an opportunity.

On the journey toward your dream, obstacles are inevitable but those who achieve their dreams are adept at not just recognising problems but also envisioning solutions and employing creative problem-solving strategies. Remarkably, many of the world's greatest inventions stemmed from solutions to problems encountered.

Consider the tale of a salesman facing a malfunctioning pen while closing a deal. Frustrated, he resolved to create a pen that would reliably write whenever needed, leading to the creation of the Waterman Pen, renowned for its excellence.

Each problem harbours the potential for discovering a solution. Thus, problems should be viewed as opportunities rather than impediments on the path to your dream. While trials are anticipated, unnecessary emotional baggage like resentment and bitterness can weigh us down and undermine our pursuit of our dreams.

A husband once queried his wife about her persistent references to the past, to which she replied, "I have forgiven and forgotten, but I want you to remember that I have forgiven and forgotten." While it may be challenging to erase memories, it is possible to refrain from dwelling on them excessively.

As psychologist Archibald Hart noted, "The memory may be there, but the sting is gone." Jesus also advised in Matthew 5:44 to "do good to them that hate you," suggesting that traveling light, free from the burdens of resentment and bitterness, leads to a more joyful journey toward realising your dream.

What potential solution can you identify for a problem you're currently facing?

I personally challenge you to embrace the belief that God has a grander vision for your life than you've ever imagined. A vision of divine proportions will propel you forward! It will infuse your mornings with purpose and ignite your days with meaning.

In his book, "Dare to Dream," John Maxwell asserts: "Daring dreams can accomplish remarkable feats. Daring dreams have revolutionised the world. Galileo dared to dream of exploring the cosmos and invented the first telescope. Lindbergh dared to dream and soloed across the Atlantic Ocean. Ford dared to dream, as did Ray Kroc, John F. Kennedy, and Martin Luther King, Jr. Daring dreams changed the course of history. However, there is a distinction between a daring dream and a mere daydream. One inspires and propels you forward. The other is nothing more than idle wishful thinking. Daring dreams are worth fighting for, while daydreams only make you want to doze off."

Our magnificent God is the source of dreams, and He has crafted a vision tailor-made for you.

1 Corinthians 2:9 declares, "No eye has seen, no ear has heard, and no mind has conceived what God has prepared for those who love Him."

God's love for you is so profound that He has envisioned a dream for you that will surpass your wildest expectations if you dare to seize it!

A Swedish Diplomat named Dag Hammarskjold once remarked, "Never measure the height of a mountain until you have reached the summit. Then you will realise how low it appeared."

What divine vision is stirring in your heart?

DESPISE NOT THE SMALL THINGS

In my opinion, 2020-2022 was undoubtedly the darkest period for our generation, and at that time, life felt shrouded in darkness. Many of us were gripped by fear, uncertain of how long. the ordeal would persist. But amidst the uncertainty, we remembered that the sun always rose, and the darkness never had the final say. I found myself in the throes of adversity during the height of the pandemic, spending Christmas and New Year in the hospital while my family prayed fervently for my recovery. It was a challenging time as I grappled with my own health while worrying about my loved ones facing their own trials. The first six months of that year brought further hardship as my family dealt with multiple hospitalisations and the loss of loved ones. Despite the difficulties, I found solace in keeping busy with my studies, writing, and online preaching. However, the challenges persisted, with my wife and niece experiencing health scares and the passing of close family members. Amidst the grief and turmoil, the birth of my granddaughter brought a glimmer of joy to our lives. Throughout it all, my faith in Christ was my anchor, sustaining me through the darkest moments. As we navigated through the remainder of 2022, I was reminded of the resilience of the human spirit and the importance of leaning on faith and family in times of adversity.

I've always found comfort in "good news, bad news" tales. One such story revolves around two close friends who shared a passion for baseball. They often pondered whether there would be baseball in heaven. To resolve the question, they devised a pact: whoever passed away first would return to inform the other of the situation. Eventually, one of them passed away, fulfilling his promise by returning in the dead of night to rouse his friend. He declared, "I've got good news and bad news. The good news is, there is baseball in heaven. The bad news is, you're pitching tomorrow."

As I reflect on the journey of my life at the age of 60, I am reminded of the profound lesson encapsulated in the phrase "Despise not the small things." Just as in the tale of the two friends and the promise of baseball in heaven, the journey toward your dreams often resembles a roller-coaster ride of good and sometimes bad news.

There are highs and lows, moments of abundance and scarcity. One of the crucial elements in reaching your dreams is learning to pay attention to the small details. Jesus emphasised this principle in Luke 16:10 when he said, "If you are faithful in little things, you will be faithful in large ones." In essence, it's about thriving wherever you're planted presently. By excelling in your current responsibilities, you pave the way for future opportunities.

Consider the peculiar demand made by the rock band Van Halen during their tours: they insisted on having a bowl of M&M candies in their dressing room, with all the brown ones removed. Lead singer David Lee Roth explained this seemingly eccentric request in his book, highlighting that if this small detail was overlooked, it could lead to larger problems during production. Conversely, if this seemingly trivial matter was handled correctly, it signalled that larger issues would likely be addressed effectively too.

Similarly, on your path toward your God-sized dream, being faithful and diligent with the little you have today can unlock doors to greater opportunities tomorrow. Every investment you make today will impact what your tomorrow looks like. As I embark on the next phase of my journey, I encourage you to reflect: What small aspect of your life could you enhance today to invite greater blessings from above tomorrow?

Printed in Great Britain
by Amazon

44319650R00056